ANTONY SZMIEREK

ROADMAP

ff Faber Music

Name: ASL★

Address: ANDROMEDA SOUTHBAND

CONTENTS

INTRO
04   Rick, the Guardian of the Tower

CAST
08   The Patron Saint of Withington / Poundshop Geri Horner / Angie / Yoga Teacher

SERVICE STATION AT THE END OF THE UNIVERSE
15   Service Station at the End of the Universe
20   Rafters
25   The Great Pyramid of Stockport
28   Big Light
34   Yoga Teacher
38   Crumb
42   The Hitchhiker's Guide to the Fallacy
47   Passingthru
53   Take Me There
58   Restless Leg Syndrome
62   Crashing Up
68   Angie's Wedding

ALTERNATIVE ROUTES
76   Constantinople
77   Vapes on a Train
78   Yacht in Canary Wharf
79   Birthday Card on the Tram
80   Ecuador Steve
82   Mulch
83   ...
86   Columbo
87   Some Worries I had at the Party
88   Decorative Equestrian Bronze
89   Meteorite (Alright)

DIVERSIONS
94   365 Days Ago
95   4pm Poem
100   Impossible Square Evolution

All lyrics © 2025 by Faber Music Ltd. All rights reserved.

RICK, THE GUARDIAN OF THE TOWER

I've been accused of being 'obsessed' with two buildings this year – one in relation to my song about the Stockport Pyramid by the BBC, the other by my band over the tower at Forton Services.

We'd driven by the tower a number of times over the summers of 2023/24 and stopped only a handful. Forton isn't far from Manchester and usually we were going the other way. It was an exciting period I'll look back on fondly forever – my songs were being played on the radio, people were coming out to see us at festivals, and the band and I were all operating at varying levels of nicotine addiction. Me, chaining a Triple Mango vape incessantly, Tom working through a selection of vapes, the occasional cigarette and the very occasional secret third option. But away from the scene setting, I had fallen down a UFO research rabbit hole. The US military had recently reclassified UFOs as UAPs (Unidentified Arial Phenomena), released many credible videos of UAP sightings, and held formal *Independence Day* style briefings all but confirming the X-Files of it all. My rational mind was keeping this information firmly at arm's length, but the creative side of my brain – the side obsessively writing an album – was getting carried away. The band were forced to listen to me only semi-ironically hyperfocus on aliens for two summers straight.

Long story short, I named the album *Service Station at the End of the Universe* – another nod to Douglas Adams and a continuation on a theme I'd started before we were constantly on the road. And in mapping this place out in my head, I knew it would have to feel like a real location. It would have a tower, and it would be just like the one at Forton. I started insisting that we stop at Forton Services every time we passed (it has a Greggs! I'd beg, it's a Moto!) but the boys in the van knew full well I was after another sordid poke around the base of the tower rather than a second Belgian bun. We'd call it The UFO, and to my absolute delight once discussed how it reminded us of the hidden spaceship at the end of the 1997 blockbuster, *Men In Black*. One of the times I'd persuaded the band to stop, I met Rick.

Rick emerged from a service door at the bottom of the tower and I caught his eye. He had two gold hoop earrings in the same ear and a black Nike cap pulled firmly over his brow. I asked him who owned the tower, a really boring question he didn't know the answer to. Next, I asked him if he'd ever been up there. He admitted he had but not for a long time, saying there were quite a lot of steps. After gentle encouragement, Rick agreed to take me up there.

I was thrilled. He said he wasn't doing anything else, really. And there were quite a lot of steps. There was also quite a lot of asbestos which he has failed to mention but I didn't hold that against him.

Anyway, Rick made my dreams come true. As I climbed the spiraling concrete steps, I felt I'd fallen into the world I'd been drafting and rearranging in my head for over a year. Rick was baffled by my enthusiasm but took to his role of custodian – guardian, even – with a pride I hadn't seen in him at the bottom of the spiral staircase. I took some photos which I have included here, and which are admittedly terrible, but at the very least you too can see the view and the family of sleeping out-of-season Christmas trees at the bottom of the stairs. There were even some of the original tiles from the restaurant up there, which I said reminded me of the Daleks. Rick said he didn't know what a Dalek was.

The tower did end up on the cover of the album, inside the snowglobe bubble-universe that my asbestos addled brain conjured up and set to music. A lot of people were really happy to see it on an album sleeve, too. The Pennine Tower was a symbol to some that they were nearly home after a long journey, in the same way the Stockport Pyramid had always welcomed me. They had embroidered it into cushions, painted it, written songs about it even. How important it was to tell stories, I remember thinking. How important it was to take ordinary things and make them extraordinary.

under a motorway bridge somewhere in North London, July 2024 / credit: Charlie Cummings

CAST

THE PATRON SAINT OF WITHINGTON

fuckin… alright then
go on son, don't be shy
screaming at the telly, searching for a why
wide eyed
deep fried
fuckin go on my mate!
go on lad you fuckin tell him

there's a mural on the wall of the flat that i dwell in
one day that'll be me
hands covered in plaster, two fingers to the sky
the sacred glowing heart of the town they gentrified

POUNDSHOP GERI HORNER

just because i like to get dressed up doesn't make me anything i'm supposedly not if you don't like me then shut up this bottle of red dye cost more than a pound but you can't see past the sequins on the union jack dress everyone is too scared to wear in case they offend or cause distress the country is in at the deep end and nobody wants to jump in and save it how's that for profound we used to be great we used to be a country what happened to girl power is it got ruined by the male gaze and that fucking rat of an ex that hasn't bothered showing his face in the pub since the last christmas well viva forever viva salford viva living the-vida-fucking-loca i'll show him what he's missing if you can't handle me at my worst then you don't deserve me at my princess new nails laughing loving living bitches love to hate real girlies love to live xoxoxoxoxo

ANGIE

poetry is for bank adverts and corporate shills
i've swept floors to pay the bills and i sure as shit won't be licking the boots of those who got us into this
nobody calls me Angela but the inland revenue
i'm optimistic

protest properly rise up spray paint on fingertips Wake Up on the clock face of Big Ben, went missing, slept in a tent, home is where my Doc Martens stand and my will won't bend until i'm in your arms again

yes i'll marry you you daft sod
stop making a fuss
i saw the sign you spray painted from the top deck of the bus

made me blush

YOGA TEACHER

fuck going back to that office
in through the nose
out though the mouth
it's all incense and headstands from here on out
in through the nose
and hold…
and out through the mouth
what if they figure me out out of date certificate running late boy from the
council estate underrated overhated headstand in the park
in through the nose, out through the mouth
spine lengthening
hands on heart
thanks for being with me today
namaste

album artwork / credit: Samuel Tomson / Mushroom Music

Album Ideas

1) Yoga Teacher — Demoed ☑
2) ▓▓▓▓▓▓▓▓▓▓ (Something inspired by The Fall)
3) Angie's Wedding
4) ▓▓▓▓▓▓▓▓▓▓
5) ▓▓▓▓▓▓▓▓▓▓
6) Doing Something
7) ▓▓▓▓▓▓▓▓▓▓
8) ▓▓▓▓▓▓▓▓▓▓ (Rating)
9) Restless Leg Syndrome
10) Big Light
11) ▓▓▓▓▓▓▓▓▓▓
12) CRASHING UP
13) Meteorite (Alright)

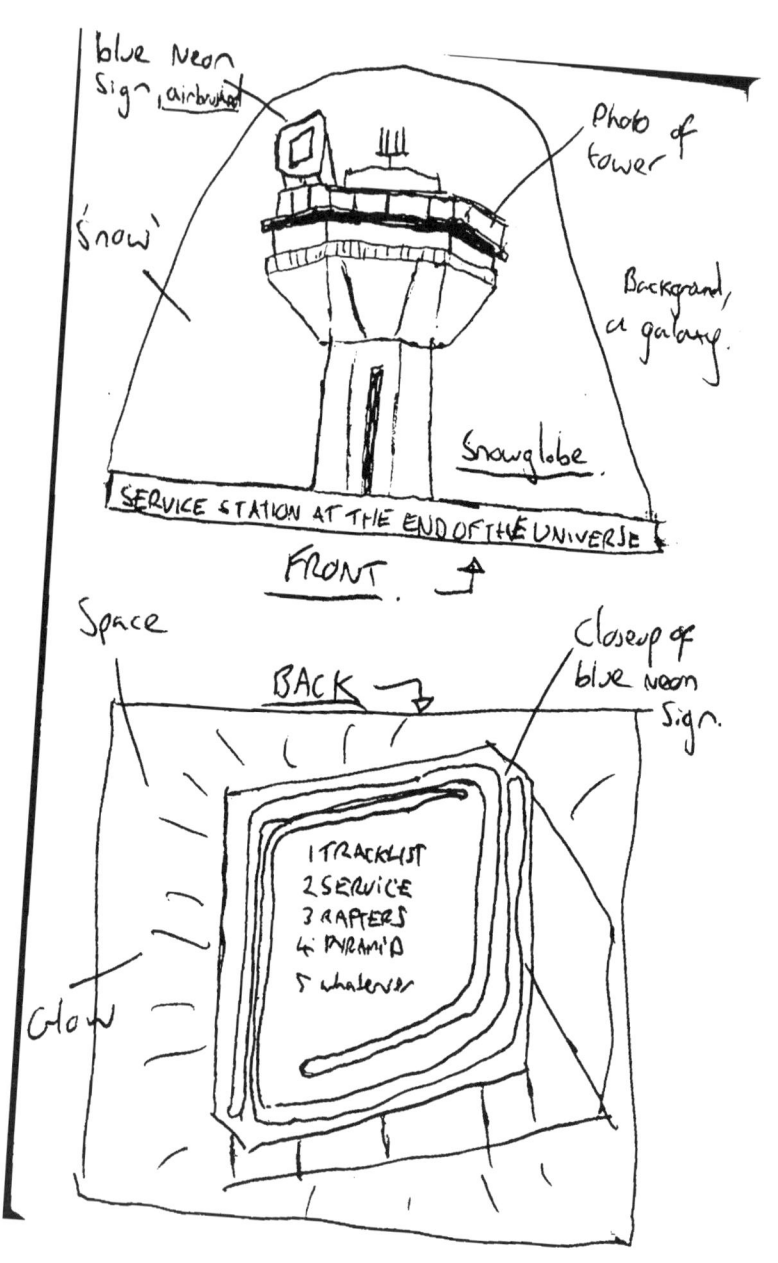

SERVICE STATION AT THE END OF THE UNIVERSE

accidentally enter through the exit sign and a
midlife crisis convertible star cruiser flies by
a brief respite from the flow of time
door slammed shut
hot dog in a hot car on the orbital road that could

automatic doors sigh dodge the wet floor sign
and the luminous gloop on the underside
a child takes a ride in a coin operated meteorite
fair play kid

half a song to the right and i'm on the motorway bridge
straight out the 1960s
18 wheeler capsizes in my mind's eye, how's that for voyeuristic?
if they all crashed i like to think i'd be the one to fix it

group of lads getting lively
Angie's Angels maid of honour can't stop crying
everyone's dying together happily dying but crying apart forever

cleaner with a face like the Horsehead Nebula
quietly doing god's work but we were abandoned long ago
fuck around and find out

a man with a yoga mat thinks he already has
probably time to head back
past the comedown crew sitting on the floor
and a Stag Do Hulk Hogan
slip on the luminous goo and onto my back, broken
someone always moves the sign

people shuffle past past lives it's a quarter to five somewhere
in the service station at the end of the universe

all the things that you believe in
the best is yet to come
the road goes on and on

EXPLODED VIEW

SERVICE STATION AT THE END OF THE UNIVERSE

accidentally enter through the exit sign and a
midlife crisis convertible star cruiser flies by
a brief respite from the flow of time
door slammed shut
hot dog in a hot car on the orbital road that could

automatic doors sigh dodge the wet floor sign
and the luminous gloop on the underside
a child takes a ride in a coin operated meteorite
fair play kid

half a song to the right and i'm on the motorway bridge
straight out the 1960s
18 wheeler capsizes in my mind's eye, how's that for voyeuristic?
if they all crashed i like to think i'd be the one to fix it

group of lads getting lively
Angie's Angels maid of honour can't stop crying
everyone's dying together happily dying but crying apart forever

cleaner with a face like the Horsehead Nebula
quietly doing god's work but we were abandoned long ago
fuck around and find out

a man with a yoga mat thinks he already has
probably time to head back
past the comedown crew sitting on the floor
and a Stag Do Hulk Hogan
slip on the luminous goo and onto my back, broken
someone always moves the sign

people shuffle past past lives it's a quarter to live somewhere
in the service station at the end of the universe

< All iCloud   29 April 2023 at 11:14

stag do hulk hogan

We find ourselves pulling off a busy motorway for a brief respite from the flow of time. It's been a long day to wherever we're going, and everyone we've ever met or might meet have congregated at The Service Station at the End of the Universe.

It's a sort-of stream of consciousness roll call at the beginning of the album that sets the scene and introduces us to the characters that exist in this bubble universe – a hen party, a young couple in love, a yoga teacher. Sonically it leans into the 90s, rave adjacent guitar music I used as a rough palette when writing and ultimately the feeling should be thus: a service station is a place where people from every walk of life cross paths on the way to or back from *something*. It's a liminal space (honestly lost count of how many times I've said that in writing this) which ultimately is a place to facilitate an escape or a homecoming. They are special and sacred and full of burgeoning mythologies. I sort of imagined my service station as this brutalist concrete structure with little portals inside akin to the paintings in *Super Mario 64*.

Fun fact: I recorded this in Bristol with my dear friend Max and the only thing I didn't have in place (lyrically) was the final sung refrain. I had 'all the things that you believe in' bouncing around my head and went into his back garden to find the next line. For a while it wouldn't come, until I overheard his elderly neighbour on the phone deliver 'the best is yet to come' to whoever was on the other end. Seems the song already existed, and I just had to be patient and wait for the rest of it to arrive.

'Rafters' video shoot, June 2024 / credit: Jamie Lee Culver

RAFTERS

the bass shakes loose a single piece of confetti from the rafters
the ghost of the party the night before
and you're the only one who notices
as it catches the light
you did say you were looking for a sign
and this might be it
spinning out over a first kiss
dodging a thrown pint pot and recalibrating it's ecliptics
she leans in
we're gonna miss that last train
birthday surprise, hollowed out cardboard cake with a stripogram inside
damp flecks collected on church steps
it was quite the entrance, they all said

i worked out the meaning
of everything
i used to get by so easy
now i'm crumbling
and i learned how to forget it
when i watched that paper square
come dancing from the ceiling
and my doubts just disappeared

it was either the first or the last of its kind
you either jump the gun or you take a lifetime to decide
don't say i didn't warn ya
the patron saint of Withington tries it on with a poundshop Geri Horner
and it's all of us
that little paper square
bad timing incarnate
too little too late
falling from the rafters
you're here right now doesn't matter where you're going after
if your mate jumped off a cliff you wouldn't try and hit the ground faster?
exactly
this one's for those who turned left and kept their head, thanks for asking

i worked out the meaning
of everything
i used to get by so easy
now i'm crumbling
and i learned how to forget it
when i watched that paper square
come dancing from the ceiling
and my doubts just disappeared

and all of a sudden there's this natural light pouring through the windows
we're alive amongst the dust
i am you and you are one of us
and nothing has to mean anything

i worked out the meaning
of everything
i used to get by so easy
now i'm crumbling
and i learned how to forget it
when i watched that paper square
come dancing from the ceiling
and my doubts just disappeared

Antony Szmierek

EXPLODED VIEW

RAFTERS

the bass shakes loose a single piece of confetti from the rafters
the ghost of the party the night before
and you're the only one who notices
as it catches the light
you did say you were looking for a sign
and this might be it
spinning out over a first kiss
dodging a thrown pint pot and recalibrating it's ecliptics
she leans in
we're gonna miss that last train
birthday surprise, hollowed out cardboard cake with a stripogram inside
damp flecks collected on church steps
it was quite the entrance, they all said

i worked out the meaning
of everything
i used to get by so easy
now i'm crumbling
and i learned how to forget it
when i watched that paper square
come dancing from the ceiling
and my doubts just disappeared

it was either the first or the last of its kind
you either jump the gun or you take a lifetime to decide
don't say i didn't warn ya
the patron saint of Withington tries it on with a poundshop Geri Horner
and it's all of us
that little paper square
bad timing incarnate
too little too late
falling from the rafters
you're here right now doesn't matter where you're going after
if your mate jumped off a cliff you wouldn't try and hit the ground faster?
exactly
this one's for those who turned left and kept their head, thanks for asking

eaning

easy

to forget it
at paper square
n the ceiling
t disappeared

there's this natural light pouring through the windows
t the dust
re one of us
mean anything

eaning

easy

to forget it
at paper square
n the ceiling
t disappeared

If we did find out the answers to life's big questions – why are we here? What happens after we die? What is our purpose? Would we ever truly be able to accept them? I think we'd struggle. And in believing that, then isn't life just looking for tiny moments that make everything feel worthwhile?

I was at a gig at Manchester's New Century Hall and noticed a single piece of confetti falling from the ceiling after a particularly violent bass note. It seemed to fall at a pace slower than everything around it, caught in its own time and space slipstream and going unnoticed by everyone else. I thought it was this beautiful, layered metaphor for living – not dissimilar to the lyrics of another of my songs 'Twist Forever': "we're all just hurtling towards the ground anyway he'd just get there quicker than me or you / pressure off, nothing to lose". It didn't seem to care that it was going to hit the ground, and everyone at the gig too was locked in the moment, arms aloft, in love with living.

So the song became much more positive, more danceable and euphoric, but still with those existential questions at the heart of it. Of course, when it came to debuting this song for the first time live, this time at our own gig at New Century Hall, a single piece of confetti did fall from the rafters. Right on cue.

SONNET 404 (RAFTERS)

Here's a verse that didn't make it:

and as you watch it fall you wonder
what's worse:
everything happening at once or nothing ever happening at all?

the others have been swept away
or carried home on the bottom of battered soles from the party yesterday

but this tiny square of paper waited
and like that film from the 80s
with the ticker-tape parade
got to live out another perfect day
confetti canon
great escape

'Great Pyramid' video shoot, June 2024 / credit: Zak Watson

THE GREAT PYRAMID OF STOCKPORT

i'm Indiana Jones you're that big polystyrene boulder
is this what you said you'd be when you fantasised about getting older?
left lane's slow the right one's for taking over
your ghost hogs the middle lane
i said i'd call on thursday
but i never
too much grind not enough rise
i swear i almost broke through last night

there's only so many times i can simulation theory myself out of lunch
pub quiz question seven just a hunch:
Cleopatra lived closer to the France '98 world cup
than the construction of the pyramids
you gotta wake up

you get one life live it
in the valley of the kings
motivationally speaking
you got everything you need

and i've seen a pyramid
they built one in Stockport
a reincarnated insurance headquarters now an Indian restaurant
and the possibilities are endless
if you can imagine it can exist
imagine what the Pharaohs could have done with a four day working week
and a three-fingered Twix

Stockport council abandoned their valley of the kings
but i'll never abandon you
god bless those big black squares we keep in the corner of the room
and remember:
you can do anything
and if they can then you can too

you get one life live it
in the valley of the kings
motivationally speaking
you got everything you need

EXPLODED VIEW

THE GREAT PYRAMID OF STOCKPORT

i'm Indiana Jones you're that big polystyrene boulder
is this what you said you'd be when you fantasised about getting older?
left lane's slow the right one's for taking over
your ghost hogs the middle lane
i said i'd call on thursday
but i never
too much grind not enough rise
i swear i almost broke through last night

there's only so many times i can simulation theory myself out of lunch
pub quiz question seven just a hunch:
Cleopatra lived closer to the France '98 world cup
than the construction of the Pyramids
you gotta wake up

you get one life live it
in the valley of the kings
motivationally speaking
you got everything you need

and i've seen a pyramid
they built one in Stockport
a reincarnated insurance headquarters now an Indian restaurant
and the possibilities are endless
if you can imagine it can exist
imagine what the Pharaohs could have done with a four day working week
and a three-fingered Twix

Stockport council abandoned their valley of the kings
but i'll never abandon you
god bless those big black squares we keep in the corner of the room
and remember,
you can do anything
and if they can then you can too

you get one life live it

28 July 2023 at 05:26

every pharaoh has his pyramid scheme

This idea was one of those that very quickly took on a life of its own. Originally it was called 'Motivational Speaker' and was this full-on parody of inspirational quotes and self-help writing. That did all eventually stay in the chorus, but the best ideas were the ones about this huge blue pyramid in Stockport, and what I thought it told us about human ambition and legacy. The idea that this could have been a mundane office block designed to house an insurance company but instead ended up this colossal, abandoned landmark just wouldn't leave me alone. When I started digging into it, I found this sprawling modern myth – some people suspected it was cursed, there were plans for an entire 'Valley of the Kings' shopping district at one point, and it was about to be resurrected as an Indian restaurant. The song naturally began to revolve around this instead, and 'Motivational Speaker' was mostly left behind.

For a long time, it had meant coming home, as we passed it on the motorway when coming back from a family holiday there would be yelps from the car. I hear people point it out from their seat as their flight approaches Manchester Airport. It's a special, silly, majestic thing that sums up the whole record. Life is to be romanticised. You must mythologise the everyday, the ordinary, and make it something more.

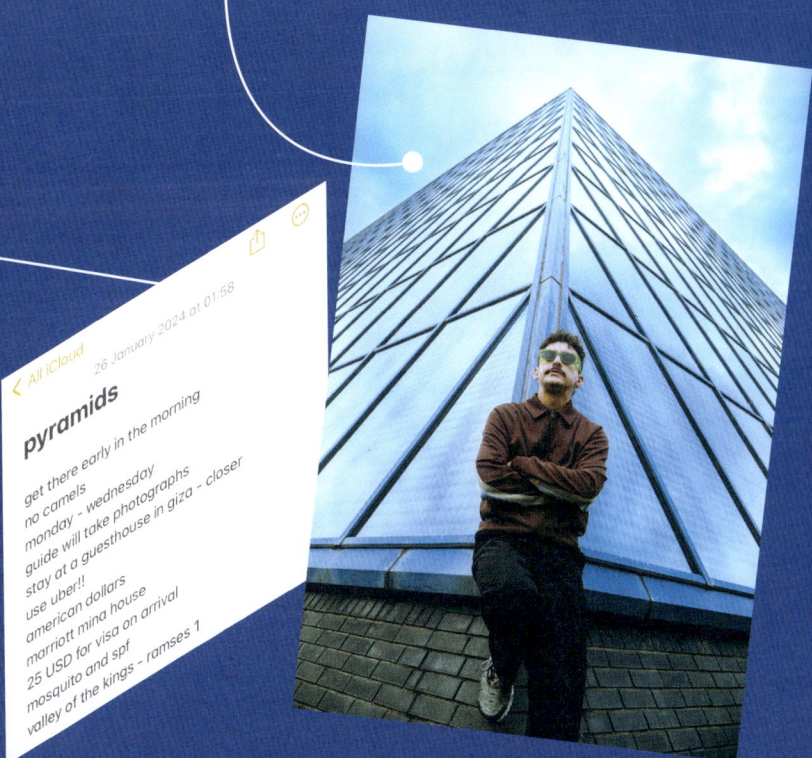

All iCloud   26 January 2024 at 01:58

pyramids

get there early in the morning
no camels
monday - wednesday
guide will take photographs
stay at a guesthouse in giza - closer
use uber!!
american dollars
marriott mina house
25 USD for visa on arrival
mosquito and spf
valley of the kings - ramses 1

Great Pyramid of Stockport, June 2024 / credit: Zak Watson

BIG LIGHT

postcode sent with a kiss
live location, north circular
starts to rain
have you seen this?
no reply 3 minutes
leg starts to bounce
crack the window a bit
good to be out of the house
at least

and when you opened the door i knew
not seen you since August
borrowed sunglasses
late afternoon
ironically synchronised dance moves
i kissed you under the moon
i thought
but it was actually just one of those big bright lights

and would you believe me?
if i said that i fell in love
i recognised the feeling
i knew you were enough
i've been talking quietly
if i believe will you believe?

you remind me of someone i wish i met
in a past life
two cold teas on the bedside table
what kind of incense was that?
i always buy the wrong one
fall asleep together wake up with the big light on
back to back
the extractor fan in the bathroom begging for attention

and i've been telling everyone who'll listen
it's always sunny on the didsbury dozen
the hotel mirror said 'be ready for that day'
but the day i was always most ready for was this
and soon i'll write your name in big red letters on a motorway bridge
if you'll have me

and would you believe me?
if i said that i fell in love
i recognised the feeling
i knew you were enough
i've been talking quietly
if i believe will you believe?

EXPLODED VIEW

Antony Szmierek

BIG LIGHT

postcode sent with a kiss
live location, north circular
starts to rain
have you seen this?
no reply 3 minutes
leg starts to bounce
crack the window a bit
good to be out of the house
at least

and when you opened the door i knew
not seen you since August
borrowed sunglasses
late afternoon
ironically synchronised dance moves
i kissed you under the moon
i thought
but it was actually just one of those big bright lights

and would you believe me?
if i said that i fell in love
i recognised the feeling
i know you were enough
i've been talking quietly
if i believe will you believe?

you remind me of someone i wish i met
in a past life
two cold teas on the bedside table
what kind of incense was that?
i always buy the wrong one
fall asleep together wake up with the big light on
back to back
the extractor fan in the bathroom begging for attention

g everyone who'll listen
on the didsbury dozen
id 'be ready for that day'
always most ready for was this
your name in big red letters on a motorway bridge

lieve me?
love
eeling
nough
uietly
believe?

< All iCloud

sun coming up listening to van bran 3000
ringa dinga dingin

disc jockey final furlong
the next song queued coulda been there all
along
in the ether
either dance or regret it henceforth
pleased to meet ya

just one more of these and i'll settle in proper
one more early morning for a thousand early
nights and a takeaway supper
chew your ear off about the war on pop culture
not everything has to rhyme

We rejoin a young couple from the party described in 'Rafters', their love in full post-summer bloom. There's talk of late-night location sharing, hazy half-memories and mornings after. There are some clues and narrative ties to the rest of the album here – words sprayed onto motorway bridges and love over long distance. I always imagined this as a stream of messages from the passenger seat of a car.

This was born at Glastonbury in a magic hour at San Remo as the sun went down. Me, Robin and my manager Chris all sort of leaned in and said, 'we should make something that feels like this', all lost in the glow of house music and psilocybin. And so we did.

The final verse came really late in the game, after the fictionalised romance I'd been writing about started to leak into my in real life. I spent a lot of 2024 in budget hotels up and down the country and noticed that the mirrors in a certain hotel chain all had warnings about cardiac arrests with instructions on how to resuscitate loved ones on them. 'be ready for that day' they said. I tried my best to twist this into something a little less morbid.

BIG LIGHT

AND WOULD YOU BELIEVE ME?
IF I SAID THAT I FELL IN LOVE
I RECOGNISED THE FEELING
I KNEW YOU WERE ENOUGH

Verse 1

Postcode sent with a kiss
live location, North Circular
starts to rain
Have you seen this?
No reply 3 minutes
leg starts to bounce
crack the window a bit
good to be out of the house
at least

and when you opened the door I had
not seen you since August
borrowed sunglasses
late afternoon
ironically synchronised dance moves
I kissed you under the moon
I thought
but it was actually one of
those big bright lights

Verse 2

You remind me of
someone I wish I met
in a past life
two cold teas on the
bedside table
what kind of incense
is that?
I always buy the wrong
one
fall asleep together
wake up with the
big light on
back to back.
the extractor fan
in the bathroom
begs for attention

'Yoga Teacher' video shoot, November 2024 / credit: Jamie Lee Culver

YOGA TEACHER

my dad never taught me to do a headstand
you just wouldn't get it
maybe i need a stranger looking at me to be able to fall asleep
to keep guard, kinda

don't know what that shit is he's burning but it smells like home
or church
we bow, i lurch forwards
off balance or recentering

i don't have any of those baggy pants but he still loves me i'm sure of it
catch his eye
my friends joke that i've come here just to meet someone and i deny it
lyingly
on this musty borrowed PE foam mat
i'm a downward facing class traitor

but he's my yoga teacher
release
he's my yoga teacher
breathe in
hold, release

try to lose yourself, he says
too late mate i'm adrift
spine lengthened and a tense midriff

i wonder if he has children and if he'd cradle me
he probably thinks it's bad for the planet and i sort of agree
at least that's what i want him to think

lotus position on the count of four
forehead to the floor
surprisingly comfortable
accidentally make eye contact with a girl i've seen before
she lives one street over
well travelled,
her own mat and a tattoo of a compass on her ankle
i'm out here in the east shaking like a leaf
i wonder if he can tell

but he's my yoga teacher
release
he's my yoga teacher
breathe in
hold, release

there's a bit where we all just lie down
my favourite bit, down here on the ground
and he moves through us
you're never quite sure where he is
and if he picks you he massages your temples his fingers move in tiny circles
and i realise these five pound lessons won't fix me
because this is about letting go
and even here,
vinyasa flow,
i'm obsessed with being chosen
and i've still got one eye open

EXPLODED VIEW

Antony Szmierek

YOGA TEACHER

my dad never taught me to do a headstand
you just wouldn't get it
maybe i need a stranger looking at me to be able to fall asleep
to keep guard, kinda

don't know what that shit is he's burning but it smells like home
or church
we bow, i lurch forwards
off balance or recentering

i don't have any of those baggy pants but he still loves me i'm sure of it
catch his eye
my friends joke that i've come here just to meet someone and i deny it
lyingly
on this musty borrowed PE foam mat
i'm a downward facing class traitor

but he's my yoga teacher
release
he's my yoga teacher
breathe in
hold, release

try to lose yourself, he says
too late mate i'm adrift
spine lengthened and a tense midriff

i wonder if he has children and if he'd cradle me
he probably thinks it's bad for the planet and i so...
at least that's what i want him to think

the count of four
or
rtable
eye contact with a girl i've seen before
t over

tattoo of a compass on her ankle
east shaking like a leaf
tell

eacher
her

just lie down
the ground
his fingers move in tiny circles

Another song that started out life as one thing and then very quickly began to reveal a lot about myself that I hadn't intended on revealing. The yoga lessons were real, the yoga teacher was a real guy, and the feelings were indeed very confusing. Did I want this guy to like me? Did I want to be him? Did I want him to be my Dad? My lover? My best friend? There really is no way to tell when you're trying to either:

A) balance on one leg or
B) try not to fall asleep

In the end, a slightly exaggerated version of this man made it onto the record – a sort of misguided guru that appears at the service station in the beginning, lingers in the subconscious throughout, and then says a good-natured farewell at Angie's Wedding. The album is about the ridiculous things we do as human beings in order to make life meaningful, knowing where we're heading. The yoga teacher might just have cracked it, although I realised it wasn't quite for me. A downward-facing class traitor I would remain.

'Yoga Teacher' video shoot, November 2024 / credit: Jamie Lee Culver

CRUMB

i want to be a crumb in your bed
so much of your hair in the flat that if
you were found dead i'd be prime suspect
locked up
bailed out by you done up
in a fake moustache and oversized hat
laughing arm in arm as the case collapsed

if i was a crumb in your bed
no hoover would find me
we kiss in two different flavours
ambiguous orange and watermelon ice
you keep your eyes closed a second longer than i do mine
your embarrassment lost in the vapour

i think of a nice place that i can take her
one that's fun but in a clever way
i'd settle for bad tv and a takeaway but
we end up kissing in a side street
and really we could be anywhere

i wanna be a crumb in your bed
i'll be anything you want
just let me be there when you're resting your head

i take her to a pub where pensioners do karaoke
not the tiniest crumb of doubt
they say you look like a famous actress i've never for a second
fantasised about
but i spend every second thinking of you

and that feels pretty nice i can't lie
got a heart like an abandoned building
needs development and leans heavily to one side
you're the flake and i'm the 98, i'm just one away from 99
we never finished watching that documentary
takeaway pizza left untouched
bottom of that paper bag it's me and you
we're just a couple of crumbs

i wanna be a crumb in your bed
i'll be anything you want
just let me be there when you're resting your head

EXPLODED VIEW

CRUMB

i want to be a crumb in your bed
so much of your hair in the flat that if
you were found dead i'd be prime suspect
locked up
bailed out by you done up
in a fake moustache and oversized hat
laughing arm in arm as the case collapsed

if i was a crumb in your bed
no hoover would find me
we kiss in two different flavours
ambiguous orange and watermelon ice
you keep your eyes closed a second longer than i do mine
your embarrassment lost in the vapour

i think of a nice place that i can take her
one that's fun but in a clever way
i'd settle for bad tv and a takeaway but
we end up kissing in a side street
and really we could be anywhere

i wanna be a crumb in your bed
i'll be anything you want
just let me be there when you're resting your head

i take her to a pub where pensioners do karaoke
not the tiniest crumb of doubt
they say you look like a famous actress i've never for a second
fantasised about
but i spend every second thinking of you

---

pretty nice i can't lie
an abandoned building
...st and leans heavily to one side
...d i'm the 96, i'm just one away from 99
...watching that documentary
...t untouched
...er bag it's me and you
...of crumbs

...b in your bed
...want
...s when you're resting your head

⟨ All iCloud

My heart is like an abandoned building in that it will probably get turned into luxury apartments

if sits there dormant,
a volcano fast asleep,
if nobody sees it then nobody sees me

my heart is like an abandoned building
people take shelter from the rain in it

it'd be a nightmare to insure
every footstep within it risks falling through the
floorboards

Again, a love song. Honest and embarrassingly sincere, charting first dates, flavoured nicotine vapour and a pub you have probably recognised by now as Manchester's legendary *The Millstone*. I wanted this to feel a bit like Backstreet Boys if they went spoken word, via *Coronation Street*. I enjoyed the idea of the album being a series of journeys from this central hub at the Service Station, all soundtracked by this one multi-genre tape like the old *Now That's What I Call Music* compilations.

It marks the midpoint on the record and closes the more optimistic Side A in a besotted four-pint haze. If you peel away the layers there is a lot of naivety and doubt around the edges too, I think.

Alamy stock photo / credit: John Kiss

THE HITCHHIKER'S GUIDE TO THE FALLACY

is hope included in this meal deal, or?
nahhh i didn't think so
the good stuff never is
you know when you forget what you were trying to say?
well
it's like that but with everything
all the time

at least sometimes there's dancing
time's just a construct but i think we'd be pretty fucked without it...
can barely get out of bed as it is
what's on your christmas wish list?
ah mate i don't really celebrate if i'm honest, but mine's a guinness and a big bag of crisps if you're offering

if you can get me from point A to point C i'll, well...
i don't really know
but it's got to be better than this
head out the window and a solar eclipse
what's the longest you've ever held a biscuit in a tea without having to make a new one?
oh man, look how big that moon's gone
mine's a kebab and a mango flavoured Rubicon
i've trailed off again

it's a fallacy
it's all a fallacy
i'm the hitchhiker
you're a galaxy
take me away
take me away
i'm the hitchhiker
you're a galaxy

and yes, it is an unconventional way to travel
do you even like this song?
no really, you can say if you don't
everything's ironic now isn't it? post post punk
no nuance in the news
top ten things you might have missed
100,000 views
easter eggs revealed in seatbelt clicks
it's exhausting

do you think this counts as one of my five a day?
how's that for a non sequitur
just here on the left mate, that's okay
i didn't exactly think this through
never have
but look, how's everything with you?
yeah, fine i guess
not reading as many books as i used to
nah i didn't watch it
my attention span kinda vanished after the second… um
whatdyacallit

don't panic
it'll all be fine in the end
the stars just didn't align
that man holding open the door that closed he's the same one who cut in front of you in the line

it's a fallacy
it's all a fallacy
i'm the hitchhiker
you're a galaxy
take me away
take me away
i'm the hitchhiker
you're a galaxy

EXPLODED VIEW

Antony Szmierek

THE HITCHHIKER'S GUIDE TO THE FALLACY

is hope included in this meal deal, or?
nahhh i didn't think so
the good stuff never is
you know when you forget what you were trying to say?
well
it's like that but with everything
all the time

at least sometimes there's dancing
time's just a construct but i think we'd be pretty fucked without it...
can barely get out of bed as it is
what's on your christmas wish list?
ah mate i don't really celebrate if i'm honest, but mine's a guinness and a big bag of crisps if you're offering

if you can get me from point A to point C i'll, well...
i don't really know
but it's got to be better than this
head out the window and a solar eclipse
what's the longest you've ever held a biscuit in a tea without having to make a new one?
oh man, look how big that moon's gone
mine's a kebab and a mango flavoured Rubicon
i've trailed off again

it's a fallacy
it's all a fallacy
i'm the hitchhiker
you're a galaxy
take me away
take me away
i'm the hitchhiker
you're a galaxy

...conventional way to travel
...his song?
...say if you don't
...now isn't it? post post punk
...ews
...might have missed

...ed in seatbelt clicks

...ounts as one of my five a day?
...n sequitur
...t mate, that's okay
...k this through

...erything with you?

...ny books as i used to
...it
...kinda vanished after the second... um

...e end
...'t align
...pen the door that closed he's the same one who cut in front

If the last few songs had been sort of grounded, we take another little dip into sci-fi surrealism here with Side B. The only song on the record that has had a previous release, it was just too important to the overarching story to leave out. You'll notice the recording is slightly more robust than the original if you know it, and I wanted it to feel more like the version I perform live – a character I sort of embody, part Blackpool Pleasure Beach crooner, part lost millennial in the back of a taxi on a journey to outer space.

It's hard to remember how this one started, other than that it was a joke title intended to make my producer Dean laugh in the studio. An ode to underthinking, originally supposed to have a big all-singing hook, and my first real foray into *Poems To Dance To*. The song that started it all, that inadvertently named the album, recontextualised and re-recorded.
It also sort of carries my mission statement, at least for now, in the line: 'Everything's ironic now isn't it? Post-post punk' – a statement meant to reclaim sincerity in the face of irony and post modernism.

It also feels like a good time to talk about Douglas Adams. I first read 'Hitchhiker' as a kid in a caravan holiday. I remember it was the blue movie tie-in cover. It was the first book I read aimed at adults and even the first page, with its wry observations on top of huge philosophical outpourings about the meaning of it all, changed me. I wanted to write like him, I wanted to create worlds and write science fiction novels and invent my own imaginary friends. And I did, in many different forms over the years and in a number of unsuccessful steps that eventually led to this album.

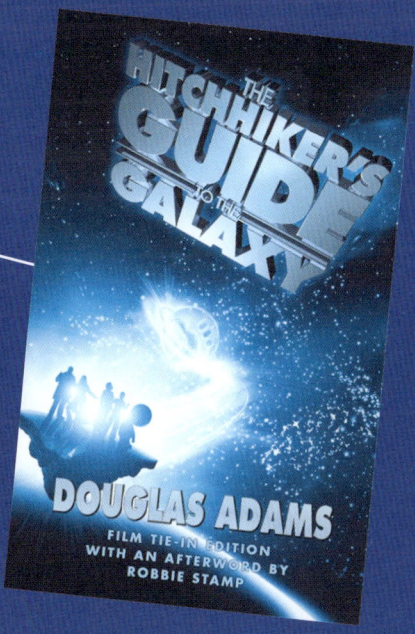

July 2024 / credit: Jamie Lee Culver

PASSINGTHRU

Kate:

this country is divided but at least all our service stations look the same

walking parallel through sliding doors into an assault course of bright lights and linoleum floors, here we are right in the middle of the inbetween

the high grade frequency of overstimulation bouncing through phone screens, fruit machines, KFC

kids sliding around in onesies – the service station renegades
here I could be anyone

heartbroken, disgraced, on the run, we all look different when we're just passing through

Me:

a voice beams down from the moon

the coordinates to happiness the hope amongst the gloom

andromeda southbound

out here we could be anyone

out here we can be new

Lyrics by Kate Ireland and Antony Szmierek

EXPLODED VIEW

Antony Szmierek

PASSINGTHRU

Kate:

this country is divided but at least all our service stations look the same

walking parallel through sliding doors into an assault course of bright lights and linoleum floors, here we are right in the middle of the inbetween

the high grade frequency of overstimulation bouncing through phone screens, fruit machines, KFC

kids sliding around in onesies – the service station renegades here I could be anyone

heartbroken, disgraced, on the run, we all look different when we're just passing through

Me:

a voice beams down from the moon

the coordinates to happiness the hope amongst the gloom

andromeda southbound

out here we could be anyone

out here we can be new

Lyrics by Kate Ireland and Antony Szmierek

I settled into the idea fairly early on that the album wouldn't have any features on it, other than obviously the collaborations with producers, the band, artists, engineers and the countless other people it takes to make a 'solo' album. But this happened very serendipitously and is one of my favourite parts of the record.

I've been friends with Kate Ireland since our open mic days and have always admired her writing and delivery. She opened for me on our first headline tour and back then I was batting around ideas for the record and when I told her I thought I'd probably call it 'Service Station…' she said she'd also written something recently about service stations, which was quite annoying, actually.

Anyway, her piece was beautiful. I always imagine it coming on over the tannoy in one of these liminal spaces, and then the narrator responding to it, almost like a character in a musical would.

Kate & Antony, July 2024 / credit: Jamie Lee Culver

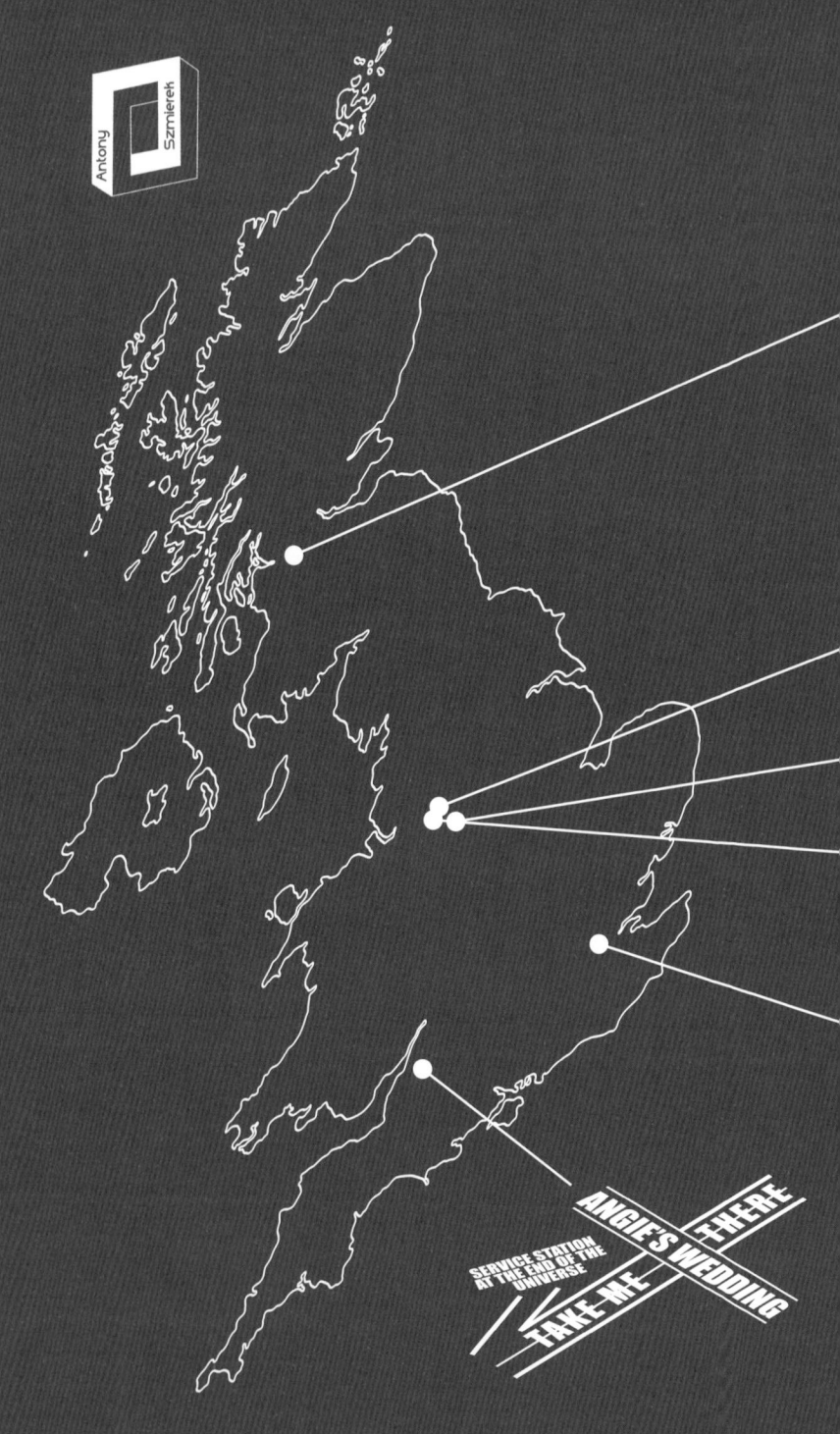

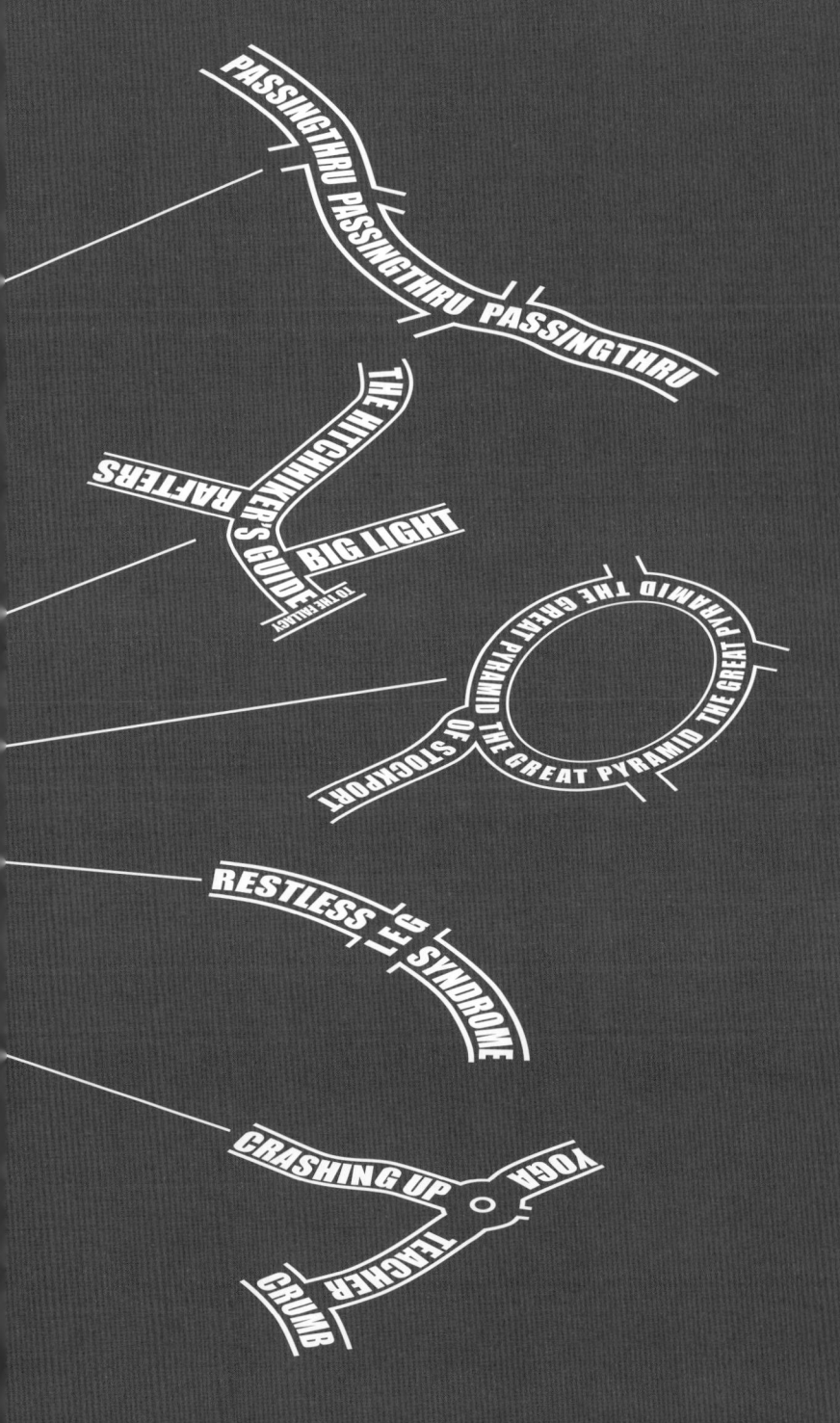

Dot to Dot, Nottingham, May 2024 / credit: Jake Haseldine

TAKE ME THERE

if you can't take me there
then nobody can

if only i knew where we were going
ain't that always the question?
there's a smiling minotaur in every direction
what's your name and what's your coinciding constellation?
mine's that one with the scales
my patience pales in comparison to how small i feel
how lost i can get
life's an explosion in a library
and everybody's shushing it

and i'll walk with ya
past a hundred wedding buffets
the last train to transcendence is facing major delays
just message me when you get back, okay?
it's been hard but i'm on the mend
you gave me a candle to see in the dark and i burned it at both ends
classic me
i trained in self-sabotage classically

if you can't take me there
then nobody can

and you know i'm here
you don't have to do this alone
we both know where we're headed
we're just walking each other home
they say all roads lead to Rome but what if they don't lead anywhere?
how am i supposed to care about a universe that doesn't care about me?
i say out loud selfishly

i'm afraid to admit i need anyone
but i've never held anything so tight as your arm
i can feel the blood pumping through it
… which is blue, i remember joyfully
it's always the little things
it's funny how you can change the connotations of something if you need to
and i need you
there i said it

always have

EXPLODED VIEW

TAKE ME THERE

if you can't take me there
then nobody can

if only i knew where we were going
ain't that always the question?
there's a smiling minotaur in every direction
what's your name and what's your coinciding constellation?
mine's that one with the scales
my patience pales in comparison to how small i feel
how lost i can get
life's an explosion in a library
and everybody's shushing it

and i'll walk with ya
past a hundred wedding bullets
the last train to transcendence is facing major delays
just message me when you get back okay?
it's been hard but i'm on the mend
you gave me a candle to see in the dark and i burned it at both ends
classic me
i trained in self-sabotage classically

if you can't take me there
then nobody can

and you know i'm here
you don't have to do this alone
we both know where we're headed
we're just walking each other home
they say all roads lead to Rome but what if they don't lead anywhere?
how am i supposed to care about a universe that doesn't care about me?
i say out loud selfishly

i'm afraid to admit i need anyone
but i've never held anything so tight as your arm
i can feel the blood pumping through it
... which is blue, i remember joyfully
it's always the little things
it's funny how you can change the connotations of something if you need to
and i need you

< All iCloud   2 January 2024 at 01:44

we're all just walking each other home

Here we have the promise of the record fulfilled – a huge party, lasers, admissions of true love, the best night of your life, everything you've ever wanted and no hint of tomorrow on the horizon. It's just you, your best friends, the love of your life and the moment flashing before your eyes.

I really just wanted to boil down One Human Life into a song here. It was originally called 'Explosion in a Library', and musically it was very difficult to finish because I was trying to glue too many ideas together. But I guess that's the point? It's a little messy but it's fun and a little sad and it's everything at once. To accurately describe it I'd need to ignore punctuation entirely and just write loads of adjectives down as quickly as possible.

There are clues about where we're headed – burnout, regret, doubt – but the music is so uplifting you just sort of forget about those more confronting lyrics in the beginning. The music becomes this Class A substance that eclipses the deeper sentiment. It's funny how you can change the connotations of something if you need to.

Dot to Dot, Nottingham, May 2024 / credit: Jake Haseldine

New Century Hall, March 2023 / credit: Max Stone

RESTLESS LEG SYNDROME

again i tricked my body into dancing all night
oh yeah here we go again i tell myself in the early daylight
the sky looks bigger and it's a different shade of blue
miserable little England framed
on the surface skirting me and you
couldn't quite get the last stamp off my wrist and now look, i've got two
not quite aligned though i suspect the bouncer did try, just like we all do

left leg almost entirely numb now, never wanted to play football more in my whole entire life
laser quest, moonwalk, spin class – anything but rest – trampoline, pedalo past Peterhead from Aberdeen to Inverness
slide my hand from underneath her chalk coloured hair and move from the door to the stairs
i'm stretching my legs in the comfort of the darkness and scratching the dry skin on the back of my neck, unaware
wide awake, laughable form
purple light of the morning adorning the walls, i'm yawning, outside a fox calls and the leaves continue to fall
fall, fall away

some people are still out i think, some are jogging, arguing, fucking, placing careful calorie controlled meal prep into a tupperware box and a branded rucksack ready to do nothing
there'll be a word for that in German
in the movies people only use their inhaler when they're nervous
i hate that shit
if i wait another ten years to have children then i'll never meet my grandkids
not sure if that's something i'm completely fine with
never been that good at perfect timing

and that's me about to spiral
when out of the darkness your arms close around my waist and you don't
even notice the dry skin on my neck or the look on my face or how sometimes
i suspect i am, in fact, just a waste of space

it's simply come back to bed
ok, i said and ok i said again
put me down, take me to the vets
you know how it gets
i'm just stretching my legs

all the places i've been
all the times that i've been low
i've been feeling restless
but i'll never let you go

EXPLODED VIEW

RESTLESS LEG SYNDROME

again i tricked my body into dancing all night
oh yeah here we go again i tell myself in the early daylight
the sky looks bigger and it's a different shade of blue
miserable little England framed
on the surface skirting me and you
couldn't quite get the last stamp off my wrist and now look, i've got two
not quite aligned though i suspect the bouncer did try, just like we all do

left leg almost entirely numb now, never wanted to play football more in my
whole entire life
laser quest, moonwalk, spin class – anything but rest – trampoline, pedalo
past Peterhead from Aberdeen to Inverness
slide my hand from underneath her chalk coloured hair and move from the
door to the stairs
i'm stretching my legs in the comfort of the darkness and scratching the dry
skin on the back of my neck, unaware
wide awake, laughable form
purple light of the morning adorning the walls, i'm yawning, outside a fox calls
and the leaves continue to fall
fall, fall away

some people are still out i think, some are jogging, arguing, fucking, placing
careful calorie controlled meal prep into a tupperware box and a branded
rucksack ready to do nothing
there'll be a word for that in German
in the movies people only use their inhaler when they're nervous
i hate that shit
if i wait another ten years to have children then i'll never meet my grandkids
not sure if that's something i'm completely fine with
never been that good at perfect timing

...ut to spiral
...rkness your arms close around my waist and you don't
...y skin on my neck or the look on my face or how sometimes
...act, just a waste of space

...ck to bed
...said again
...me to the vets
...ets
...my legs

...been
...ve been low
...stless
...u go

< All iCloud 29 October 2023 at 01:13

the worlds biggest cigarette crew

Antony Szmierek

And now the inevitable comedown. I originally wrote this poem in a sort of dissociative state the day after a particularly big dance at Salford's White Hotel. We left when it was daylight and I travelled home with the commuters – one of those mornings. Anyway, these words were bouncing round my head when I came round from a sleep of some design, I suppose, and I felt properly compelled to write them down. There's lots in here: loneliness, disassociation, eczema, self-consciousness, fears about the future – all the classics. The line about never meeting my grandkids came to me as I was driving to work the following day and literally forced me off the road.

For all the characters in the album, this is where I introduce myself into the narrative and sit alongside them. It's quite meta which I said three songs ago I was going to avoid doing but the lyrics of this will tell you how much of a hypocrite I think I am.

There is a hopeful resolve though – at this time it was a yearning for someone who didn't exist yet. I was imagining being happy and stable and satisfied. I have been very, very lucky since this poem first came to me, but my real life Restless Leg Syndrome has only gotten worse. I think it's wear and tear on my hip. At least the ennui has eased off slightly.

CRASHING UP

ever thought about getting to know yourself?
well i did and sometimes i wish i didn't
you can't cancel plans on the voice in your head
sometimes it's mine, sometimes it's someone else
and it's not even an actor that i like

i guess that's kinda self-destructive
when you ask i'll say i'm only messing
open up my chest and you'll find a big red button
and a warning not to press it
but the text has faded off it's just a guide it's window dressing

and i still need you
i'm torn apart i just needed a friend
do i want to?
i've fallen down i'm crashing up again

stepped out
called the saviour complex anonymous hotline
and got the dial tone
guess you can't save everyone
especially if you've not been to the dentist in four years
and you're allergic to saving money

searching symptoms online
why do i feel so tired all the time?
starting to miss the H in my ADHD
worry all my friends secretly hate me
and i'll show them because, well
i couldn't even look in the mirror this morning

had a shower with the light off
couldn't face looking at my skin
thought it best to leave the flat with false confidence
than crippling embarrassment

i hate the sound of my own voice
i hate the sound of my own voice
life's just an invoice you can't cash in
clothes soaking wet from a dip in Big Guilt River
chucked all my pennies in but still no wishes richer

and i can't stop looking at that picture
what goes down must come crashing up
but i wish the crashing would come crashing quicker
i just know that you'll be fine and that i'll be even better

and i still need you
i'm torn apart i just needed a friend
do i want to?
i've fallen down i'm crashing up again

i do appreciate you being here
i'm just knackered, you know
there's a lot going on
and yeah, i'm doing a lot of talking but
i'm sick of the sound of myself, you know
i'm sorry i never got back to ya
but i'm trying

EXPLODED VIEW

CRASHING UP

ever thought about getting to know yourself?
well i did and sometimes i wish i didn't
you can't cancel plans on the voice in your head
sometimes it's mine, sometimes it's someone else
and it's not even an actor that i like

i guess that's kinda self-destructive
when you ask i'll say i'm only messing
open up my chest and you'll find a big red button
and a warning not to press it
but the text has faded off it's just a guide it's window dressing

and i still need you
i'm torn apart i just needed a friend
do i want to?
i've fallen down i'm crashing up again

stepped out
called the saviour complex anonymous hotline
and got the dial tone
guess you can't save everyone
especially if you've not been to the dentist in four years
and you're allergic to saving money

searching symptoms online
why do i feel so tired all the time?
starting to miss the H in my ADHD
worry all my friends secretly hate me
and i'll show them because, well
i couldn't even look in the mirror this morning

had a shower with the light o[ff]
couldn't face looking at my s[elf]
thought it best to leave the fl[at]
than crippling embarrassment [...]

[right column, partially visible:]
my own voice
my own voice
you can't cash in
from a dip in Big Guilt River
nnies in but still no wishes richer

king at that picture
ust come crashing up
hing would come crashing quicker
'll be fine and that i'll be even better

needed a friend

crashing up again

being here
you know

a lot of talking but
nd of myself, you know
t back to ya

< All iCloud

saviour complex anonymous hotline

if you need something doing
then do it yourself
if i think about helping you
then i don't have to think about how much i'm
not helping myself

< All iCloud 14 May 2023 at 03:37

crashing up

everything that goes down
must come crashing up

Again, we're dealing with all that came before. All of these latent insecurities that have come to light are being dealt with here, and it's still me – Antony – narrating this one. If 'Take Me There' fulfils that promise of a fictional rave somewhere beyond the Service Station then this song is the emotional pay off – huge guitars and junglist loops and all. It's me dealing with what I've learned about myself and owning up to it, making peace with who I am and how much time I have left.

This came quite early in the recording process and I really wanted to make that huge final song that so many bands have in their live set. The climax of this is one of my favourite parts of the record and I always enjoy people's reaction when the screaming guitars come in. I've never been married to a particular genre and love that this feels like a couple at once.

Crashing Up ⇧

AND I STILL NEED YOU...
I'M TORN APART I JUST NEEDED A FRIEND
DO I WANT TO?
I'VE FALLEN DOWN I'M CRASHING UP AGAIN.

'Angie's Wedding' video shoot, January 2025 / credit: Zak Watson

ANGIE'S WEDDING

where's everyone heading on a day like this? bank holiday Sunday marry me, Angie in big red letters, I wonder if she did? 'no war but class war' on the motorway bridge, love spelled backwards on the next, police tape encircles flowers, a little note reads 'no regrets'

a bedsheet tapestry hangs 'support our local lad, he's on reality TV', put your head on my shoulder just try to get some sleep, police witness pleas, sun angrily beats, 100 million chevrons away
i'll be fine I just need you to stay, okay?

and i hope Angie did get married and that local lad became the influencer he always thought he wanted to be, 'happy 13th birthday Alfie' reads another sign on a lay-by and they're all celebrating somewhere together in my mind's eye, the doers and the dreamers, in an working men's club watching Angie cut her cake
a yoga teacher that used to rave and a former spice girl that married a saint
a ticker-tape parade for the ones who made it
you can be my plus one if you let me hold you naked
or
by your ankles over the motorway
sign our names in aerosol and paint
me and you and Angie we're all the same

it's the wedding of the century
i don't know how to feel
all the things we were meant to be
in the moment revealed

and i hope she made it
coz not many of us do
and i can't explain it
you just light up the room

and i hope she made it
and i hope she made it

EXPLODED VIEW

ANGIE'S WEDDING

where's everyone heading on a day like this? bank holiday Sunday marry me, Angie in big red letters, I wonder if she did? 'no war but class war' on the motorway bridge, love spelled backwards on the next, police tape encircles flowers, a little note reads 'no regrets'

a bedsheet tapestry hangs 'support our local lad, he's on reality TV', put your head on my shoulder just try to get some sleep, police witness pleas, sun angrily beats, 100 million chevrons away
i'll be fine I just need you to stay, okay?

and i hope Angie did get married and that local lad became the influencer he always thought he wanted to be, 'happy 13th birthday Alfie' reads another sign on a lay-by and they're all celebrating somewhere together in my mind's eye, the doers and the dreamers, in an working men's club watching Angie cut her cake
a yoga teacher that used to rave and a former spice girl that made it
a ticker-tape parade for the ones who made it
you can be my plus one if you let me hold you naked
or
by your ankles over the motorway
sign our names in aerosol and paint
me and you and Angie we're all the same

it's the wedding of the century
i don't know how to feel
all the things we were meant to be
in the moment revealed

and i hope he made it
coz not many of us do
and i can't explain it
you just light up the room

and i hope she made it
and i hope she made it

how much would it cost to sample madonna

The record was always going to end at either a wedding or a wake. There's something so inescapably human about both of those ceremonies, and I always knew that the journey from the 'Service Station at the End of the Universe' would end at one or the other.

The decision for it to be a wedding was informed by the rest of the writing. I'd surprised myself with how dark and introspective I'd gone with some of the songs on Side B and ultimately, at this point in my career anyway, wanted to end on a hopeful note. So all of the characters meet at a wedding – the real question was whose? And the idea of the 'doers and the dreamers' came from some graffiti on a motorway bridge near my mum's house in Hyde which read 'No War But Class War'. I cast my mind back to all of the motorway graffiti I'd seen over the years, hanging over laybys and bridges, memorials, pleas for witnesses, jokes, adverts, and a marriage proposal. It just felt like the perfect way to sum it all up – these grand swings of hopefulness in a mostly hopeless world. People truly making the most of it. People coming together to change things.

So we get the wedding, and this final burst of triumphant Madchester piano just for a few seconds. I like to think of the wedding as a sort of Valhalla, a place beyond where people go to be together. A place where all the grand swings paid off.

'Angie's Wedding' video shoot, January 2025 / credit: Zak Watson

ALTERNATIVE ROUTES

CONSTANTINOPLE

at the party I call you by your old name
like Constantinople
and in front of so many people

privately we think about how funny it is that we used to call each other that
and how our name sounded a bit like Bombay
which is now Mumbai

the party rages and I call you by your real name
twice more, loudly
to prove you are no longer occupied
like St. Petersburg

nobody but you notices

VAPES ON A TRAIN

A storm rolls in and Lynne, our conductor, informs us that the train is three times over capacity. Despite this, there is a good-natured atmosphere of forced camaraderie as people are forced into close quarters combat. Eyes are rolled and quips exchanged.

We are going to Scotland. A child watches *King Kong* on his iPad and exclaims in joy when he sees Nick Fury. His Dad tells him this is Samuel L. Jackson, and that he is an actor from *Snakes on a Plane*. And now in my head I am playing a game in which I try to pitch myself possible sequels, just to pass the time. Of course they have to rhyme, these unavoidable and deeply silly Shapes in my Brain.

Snakes are a Pain, I think.
Snakes are so Lame, Snakes are to Blame, even.

An hour later and Storm Dennis is kicking the *fuck off*. A stag do reaches maximum slur. They have a novelty hip flask the size of an Argos catalogue. A penguin is sent to 'The Exclusion Zone' for swearing, which is in the little airlock where the doors are. Others join him and they huddle together. I pass through a cloud of raspberry flavoured mist on my way to the toilet when it hits me – Vapes on a Train – just as I was hitting a creative lull. I smile and inhale secondhand vapour, rocking side to side as I empty my bladder.

A seven year old boy strikes up a conversation when I return. I ask him what his favourite planet is and he replies, knowingly, that it is Uranus. Japes in the Rain, man. I like his style. He goes on to tell me that wind speeds reach up to 900km/hour out there, and that the winds outside the carriage are absolutely nothing to worry about. On Uranus, Storm Dennis would be a nobody but here the Stakes are Insane. Undoubtedly.

Our train trundles into Edinburgh battered and bruised. The stag have become a charity choir and are in full voice singing a strangely accomplished version of 'California Dreamin'. We join in, me and the kid's parents, with absolute sincerity. A flying branch hits the window to the line 'All the leaves are brown / And the sky is grey' and we all laugh.

To some this would understandably be hell on earth. A Snake in the Rain on a circular track, revolving and banking and eating its own tail forever, never looking back. I am not so sure. I ask the kid to think of something that rhymes with Snakes on a Plane and he eventually comes up with Steaks on Snakes, which doesn't work at all. But I forgive him.
We alight.

YACHT IN CANARY WHARF

as the DLR slides through the bowels of a skyscraper
i notice
that there is a yacht moored in Canary Wharf

like the bird from the idiom
caged
it seems to be alerting us to the presence
of imperceptible poisonous gasses

it bobs audaciously on the surface
like Mercaptan,
the artificial gas smell that they put in ovens

i lose sight of it
but nobody else seems to have noticed

BIRTHDAY CARD ON THE TRAM :)

you are closer to 100 than the day you were born
open brackets haha close brackets
smiley face

ECUADOR STEVE

There's a man who goes by the name 'Guilty Feet' because, like the song, he's got no rhythm. A man who works as a talent scout called 'Sex Tape' because he makes people famous. Me? I'm stuck with Ecuador Steve. Forever Ecuador Steve all because of a question I got wrong on a quiz show four years ago.

But I've moved on since then.

I really have. I married my second (and favourite) wife and I'm doing well at work. We're happy and are planning a river cruise next summer. For a while though, all I could think about was:

Which South American country is also the name of a 1997 single by 'Sash!'?
A) Venezuela B) Peru
C) Ecuador D) Columbia

Of course I answered Columbia, didn't I? Blew my chance at half a million. And now there's a drink named after me at The Red Lion. People shout 'EK-WAH-DOR!' at me in the street. They chant the melody when I walk by. And despite me working hard to become Pub Quiz Champion four years on the bounce, Ecuador Steve is always my team name. Got to show them I'm laughing! Haha! Ha. H-

Four years later and I'm there in the hot-seat again, studio lighting boring a hole into the back of my head. Pressure on. Told my wife I'd finally slay my demons and make amends. Another right answer and I'm guaranteed twenty grand. One slip up and I'm back to drinking Ecuador Steve's in The Red Lion. But.

Angel Falls is located in which South American country?

Oh God.

A) Venezuela B) Peru
C) Ecuador D) Columbia

I'm paralysed by an anecdotal affiliation to a country I've never even visited, but I won't – can't – let it happen again. I trust my gut and answer Ecuador, pretty certain I'm sailing through. I am Ecuador Steve after all. I'm Ecuador Steve and I'm wrong and I've gone home with nothing because the answer was fucking Venezuela. It really is different when you're in the studio, like they always say.

I didn't leave the house for a month after the show went out. Genuinely never thought I'd be happy again. How can you be when an entire country is complicit in your downfall? Ecuador ruining Ecuador Steve's life. I would be buried there, I decided. I would let it swallow me whole.

Until I received a letter. There was conspiracy afoot. The person writing promised recompense. A lifeline. A second second chance.

But there were no answers inside the house I visited, not in the traditional sense. Instead I found others. There was the guy who incorrectly answered the final question on *Millionaire*. A girl who joined the 'Two-Hundred Club' on *Pointless* two shows in a row. Somebody they called 'Cuttlefish' because of an unforgivable blunder on the *Million Pound Drop*. This was Valhalla for losers. "If you want" somebody whispered, "we can just call you Steve."

MULCH

it is late summer and the leaves are yellowing
but still abundant enough to hiss oceanlike in the breeze

we should learn something from their late-stage defiance
as they watch their friends
fall one by one
into
the
mulch

■■■

here I am,
right where you left me

always waiting for you in the grey abyss between typing and its elipsis
but in that moment it flicks back to just
last seen I doubt everything I have ever known or ever been

my phone has learned to add the diaeresis to your name and my targeted
ads have all changed, which tells me that my phone is more sure of this than
either of us are

you are beautiful and I like you.
I like you more than I don't like the things I tell everyone I don't like,
the things that I have made an intrinsic part of my personality

from an undisclosed point in the future I remember reading you this poem and
ultimately I forgive myself

for what I am unsure

New Century Hall, March 2023 / credit: Max Stone

COLUMBO

today I have coffee next to a dog called
Columbo
after the famous TV detective

if my life is a whodunnit then you are the one to unravel its mysteries, I decide,
and despite my allergies I reach out to you and your unknowable wisdoms

just one more thing...
your eyes say

always the same shit with you isn't it?
I reply

SOME WORRIES I HAD AT THE PARTY

It starts because the room is too small, I think, for that many people. Also we are in the basement and the windows have heavy curtains covering them and I start to feel a bit like we're all down here waiting for the bombs to drop. I wonder if this is where I want to be when my skin is irradiated off of my bones.

I have met a lot of people at the party before and they seem to know me but I can't settle on anything interesting to say. I ask about work even though it is a Saturday. I worry that I am standing peculiarly. That I am too short. That everybody here hates me, despite the compliments and smiles.

There is an imagined pressure in which I think everybody expected me to be funnier and more entertaining than I actually am. In this situation I am an automatic disappointment to anyone I strike up a conversation with or bump into as they dance to 'Castle's in the Sky'. I am torn between dancing ironically or with sincerity. It is a battle I have waged before.

I am locked in my own head, not sure if it's better to be funny or cool. You are also. So are the two shirts at the bar. I remind myself that I am not always like this but it does not make me feel any better. I rifle through a number of plausible solutions with sweating palms:

Be honest, just like you are in the corner of your favourite pub. Close your eyes when you are dancing, like you do in your bedroom. Take five minutes in the toilet even though you don't need it or go out for a cigarette even though you don't want it. Stop worrying that you have been gone too long. That you missed the cake. There are sure to be other cakes soon and you are gluten intolerant anyway.

These are some of the worries I had at the party.
Your eyes tell me that maybe you had them too.
We wonder, frantic and apart, why we continue to put ourselves through it.

DECORATIVE EQUESTRIAN BRONZE

I heard a man say the phrase Decorative Equestrian Bronze on an auction show yesterday
when I looked up and took in the mounted dead-eyed heads and Pompeii poses I felt just like the polished horseshoe that dangled from his arms in a leather belt.
that is to say that I was confused.

but struck by just how satisfying it was to say Decorative Equestrian Bronze out loud.
I proceeded to say it so many times that I missed the valuation.

I remember that my grandma had Decorative Equestrian Bronze by the fireplace and honestly I don't think she's ever seen a horse in her life so I am surprised by her urge to commemorate their existence in polished figurines.
for they were polished,
and regularly.

but I guess there are some things we'll just never understand about each other,
I think
mumbling the words
Decorative
Equestrian
Bronze
into my glowing tablet and double chin

probably somewhere in the region of eighty to one hundred pounds.

Meteorite (Alright)

THERE WE WERE
THAT RAINED OFF SUMMER WHEN I COULDNT STOP
TALKING ABOUT UFOS
AND NO MATTER HOW UNLIKELY ALIENS SEEMED
TO BE I WAS SO BUSY I JUST WANTED
SOMETHING TO BELIEVE
MY NEW FATHER CHRISTMAS
PARTY TIME IN SOUTH MANCHESTER
MIRACULOUSLY DRY
WE LOOKED UP TO THE SKY TOGETHER AND
NOTICED THE STARS
LIKE, REALLY NOTICED FOR THE FIRST TIME

A LULL IN CONCENTRATION
WE START LAUGHING BETWEEN THE BASS BENEATH
THE CONSTELLATIONS
A LOOK ON UR FACE HALF LAUGHTER
HALF AMAZEMENT

I THINK I JUST SAW A SHOOTING STAR,
YOU'RE SAYIN

DO I GET LOADS OF WISHES NOW?

New Century Hall, July 2023 / credit: Max Stone

DIVERSIONS

‹ All iCloud

20 December 2022 at 14:27

365 days ago we were in this same place
Mad that it's like, a year ago to the day
But...anyway
Don't know how much of it you remember
We were between that left speaker and the smoking area, had our own little zone like, this little circle of light I think Joey called it

Anyway we took that picture
We've all got our sunnies on, you know the one, like, outside it's already daylight and we're holding cans of hooch coz of that private joke from that one time
All smiles, no hindsight
Yeah that's the one yeah yeah that night

4pm Poem

depending on your mood at 4pm
it could easily be dawn,
but also it could be that indistinguishable period between your first kiss with a stranger and the trudge to a taxi rank after a warehouse rave in 2009

the sky is such an ugly fucking colour at 4pm if you're not in the mood for it, let me tell you
and now I can't remember any good synonyms for grey
or 'gray' depending on where you're from on planet earth

but

on good days the sky at 4pm is parchment steeped in peach, or god shining a torch from a christmas cracker through amethyst
and you don't even need to think about the synonyms for fucking anything

nobody can picture me driving a car

13 March 2023 at 16:57

---

for someone who didn't care in the first place i sure am aching

1 April 2023 at 00:00

---

i want to go places where they fetishise my accent

17 March 2023 at 01:14

---

dandelion and murdoch

27 April 2023 at 21:39

---

we left our lubricant
on the floor by the stool
in its little sachet
that reminds me of the bonus sauce
in a pot noodle

31 March 2023 at 23:30

open casket funeral for my last set of 3am confessions

i'll pay my respects on Sunday
as is tradition
but i'll still wish i hadn't looked.
i've heard they use super glue for the mouth
just like, regular stuff

too much to destroy

if circumstances were different
your eyes say
then maybe

but there is too much to destroy

It's 3am Somewhere

Hit me with another fridge magnet chat up line
and lower your eyes
a Kubrick stare fandango
I'll be the first to admit i'm a sell out
I'm Twistiano Ronaldo
A 30 second modern myth
Jerry Seinfeld on a crucifix

under a motorway bridge somewhere in North London, July 2024 / credit: Charlie Cummings

IMPOSSIBLE SQUARE EVOLUTION

The Impossible Square logo is supposed to represent imperfection – the idea of being fallible and making mistakes. I liked that it looked like a snake eating its own tail and the obvious optical illusion.

In the initial design I'd tried filling in the colours using MS Paint, and ended up with this glitchy, pixilated version. This only added to the sense of chasing impossible perfection that had made me choose the square in the first place, so I kept it.

Once we started getting booked for festivals big enough to let us have our own visuals on the screen behind us, we updated the logo to make it clearer and so that included my name. My friend Amy McCall finessed the final design.

In April 2023 we played two very special additional tour shows at New Century Hall in Manchester and Lafayette in London. To commemorate these shows, I headed back to MS Paint to design an Impossible Square that represented the four seasons, after my EP *Seasoning*.

At the end of 2023 I left teaching and became a full-time musician. I designed this ring with @samozanne.design to serve as a reminder of what I'd achieved. A coward's tattoo.

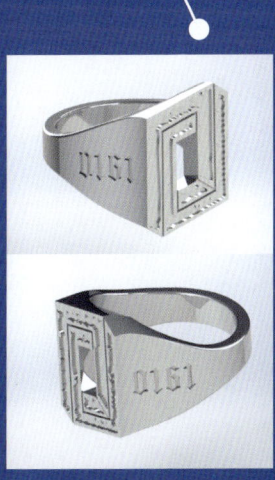

Once I'd sketched the album cover and knew Forton Services was going to take pride of place, I added a neon Impossible Square to the roof to really lay claim to the fictional place and add that important sci-fi final touch.

New Century Hall, April 2024 / credit: Adam Houghton

Copyright © Antony Szmierek, 2025

Antony Szmierek's right to be identified as the author of the lyrics reproduced in this book has been asserted.

Book design by Dominic Brookman
Edited by Lucy Holliday

With thanks to Chris Bellam at underplay music

© 2025 by Faber Music Ltd.
First published in 2025
by Faber Music Ltd.
Brownlow Yard
12 Roger Street
London WC1N 2JU

Printed and bound in
Turkey by Imago

All rights reserved.

ISBN 1 0-571-54341-3
EAN 13: 978-0-571-54341-0

Reproducing this book in any form is illegal and forbidden by the Copyright, Designs and Patents Act, 1988

To buy Faber Music publications or to find out about the full range of titles available please contact your local retailer or Faber Music sales enquiries:

Faber Music Limited, Burnt Mill,
Elizabeth Way, Harlow, CM20 2HX, England
Tel: +44 (0) 1279 82 89 82
fabermusic.com

New Century Hall, March 2023 / credit: Max Stone